Math Masters

Geometry

The Class Mural

Reason with Shapes and Their Attributes

Justine Price

NEW YORK

Published in 2015 by The Rosen Publishing Group, Inc.
29 East 21st Street, New York, NY 10010

Book Design: Mickey Harmon

Photo Credits: Cover Sebastian Duda/Shutterstock.com; p. 5 Africa Studio/Shutterstock.com; pp. 7, 15 (teacher) Ermolaev
Alexander/Shutterstock.com; pp. 7, 15 (classroom) Tanchic/Shutterstock.com; p. 11 (drawings) Anthonycz/
Shutterstock.com; p. 14 Pablo Scapinachis/Shutterstock.com; p. 18 Leah-Anne Thompson/Shutterstock.com; p. 22 Blend
Images/Shutterstock.com.

Library of Congress Cataloging-in-Publication Data

Price, Justine, author.
The class mural : reason with shapes and their attributes / Justine Price.
     pages cm. — (Math masters. Geometry)
 Includes index.
ISBN 978-1-4777-4903-6 (pbk.)
ISBN 978-1-4777-4904-3 (6-pack)
ISBN 978-1-4777-6443-5 (library binding)
1. Geometry—Juvenile literature. 2. Shapes—Juvenile literature. 3. Mural painting and decoration—Juvenile literature.
I. Title.
 QA445.5.P75 2015
 516—dc23
                              2013048657

Manufactured in the United States of America

CPSIA Compliance Information: Batch #WS15RC: For further information contact Rosen Publishing, New York, New York at 1-800-237-9932.

3 9082 12780 3354

Contents

Our Art Project   4

Circles for Everyone   6

Dividing Circles   8

Empty Spaces   14

Working with Rectangles   16

Finishing the Mural   22

Glossary   23

Index   24

Our Art Project

Art class is my **favorite** thing about school. I love to draw and paint. My art teacher, Mrs. Collins, has a big **project** for my class to do. We're painting a mural in our classroom!

A mural is a very large work of art painted directly on a wall. It takes a lot of planning and hard work to paint a mural.

My class is very **creative**. We have a lot of ideas for making our mural look beautiful! ▶

Circles for Everyone

Mrs. Collins has painted enough circles on the wall for each of us to have our own. She wants us to paint things in the circles that show who we are. This way, everyone has something that **represents** them on the mural.

If we want to paint more than 1 thing in our circle, we need to **divide** the circle into equal shares. Mrs. Collins shows us how to do that.

A circle is a round shape with no **straight** lines. However, to divide a circle into equal parts, you need to draw straight lines through the center of the circle.

Dividing Circles

I want my part of the mural to show that I love to read and play basketball. To show this, I have to divide my circle into 2 equal parts. Each of these parts is called a half.

In 1 half of my circle, I paint a book. In the other half, I paint a basketball. When I put these 2 halves together, they make a whole circle.

$$\frac{1}{2} = \textbf{one-half}$$

There are many ways to divide a circle in half. As long as the line starts on 1 side of the circle and passes straight through the circle's center, you can make 2 equal halves.

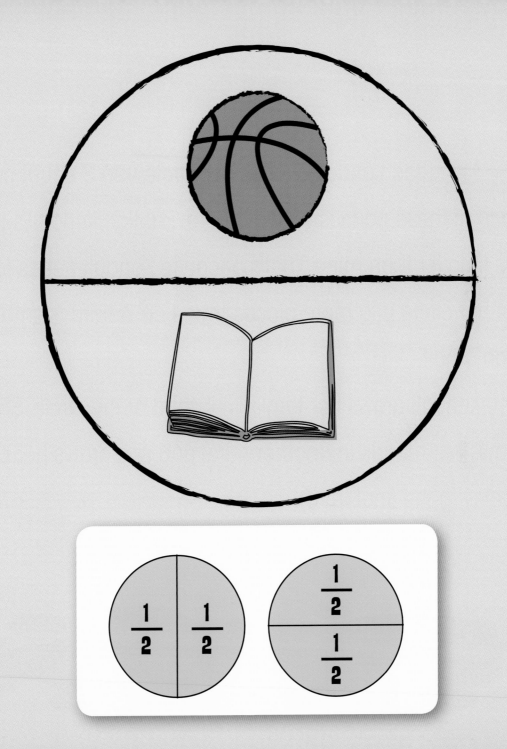

My friend Kendall divides her circle into 3 equal parts. Each of these parts is called a third. I notice Kendall's parts are smaller than mine. That's because Kendall needs to cut her circle into more pieces than I do. A third is smaller than a half.

Kendall draws her family in 1 third of the circle. She draws her friends in another third, and she draws her cat Sparky in the final third.

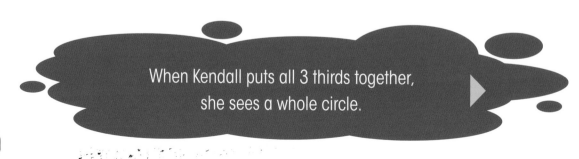

When Kendall puts all 3 thirds together, she sees a whole circle.

$\dfrac{1}{3}$ = one-third

Brayden wants to paint his favorite school subjects in his circle. He has 4 of them, so Mrs. Collins helps him divide his circle into 4 equal parts. These are called fourths. It takes 4 fourths put together to make a whole circle.

Brayden paints something different in each fourth of the circle: a music note, an addition sign, a map, and a paintbrush. Can you tell what his favorite subjects are?

Brayden first divides his circle in half. Then, he divides each half into 2 equal pieces. That makes 4 equal pieces, or 4 fourths.

$$\frac{1}{4}$$ = one-fourth

Empty Spaces

There are some spaces left on the mural for my classmates and I to paint together. The empty spaces are rectangles, which are shapes with 2 long sides, 2 short sides, and 4 equal corners. Unlike circles, rectangles are made using only straight lines.

Mrs. Collins shows us how to divide the rectangles equally. This gives everyone a chance to paint 1 more thing on our mural.

Before we paint on the mural, we practice painting on pieces of paper that are also rectangles.

Working with Rectangles

We divide the first rectangle on the mural into 2 parts. Mrs. Collins helps us make sure both halves of the rectangle are equal in size. In 1 half, the boys paint pictures of themselves. In the other half, the girls paint pictures of themselves. When we put the 2 halves together, they make a whole rectangle.

Mrs. Collins shows us 2 different ways to divide a rectangle into halves.

A rectangle can be divided in half by drawing a straight line down the middle of the shape. It can also be divided in half by drawing a line across the middle from 1 side to the other. ▶

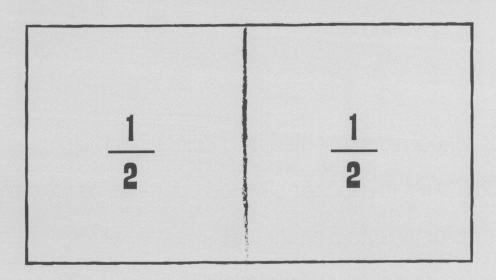

$$\frac{1}{2} = \text{one-half}$$

Our school is represented by 3 colors: blue, white, and yellow. We show these colors on our mural by dividing another rectangle into 3 equal parts.

We can divide the rectangle into thirds in 2 different ways. We can draw 2 straight lines from the top of the rectangle to the bottom. We can also draw 2 straight lines from 1 side of the rectangle to the other.

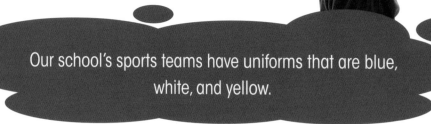

Our school's sports teams have uniforms that are blue, white, and yellow.

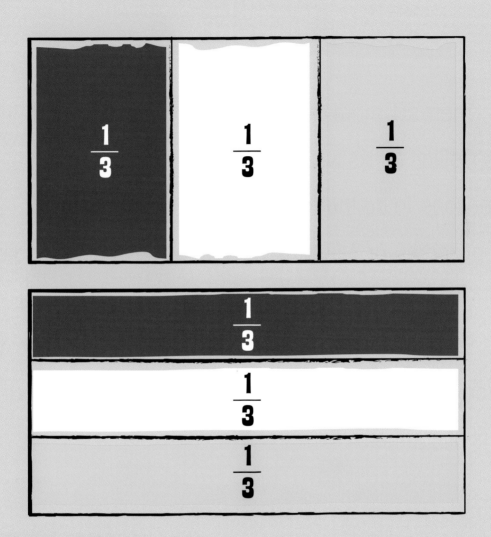

$\frac{1}{3}$ = one-third

There's 1 more rectangle left to paint on our mural. Mrs. Collins thinks we should paint it to represent the 4 seasons. To do that, we divide the rectangle into 4 equal shares, or 4 fourths. Each fourth of the rectangle represents 1 season.

First, we divide the rectangle into 2 halves. Then, we divide each half into 2 equal parts. That makes 4 equal parts altogether.

We paint 1 fourth of the rectangle white for the winter snow. Another fourth is green for the plants that grow in spring. The fourth representing summer is yellow for the sun. And the fourth representing fall is orange because leaves turn colors such as orange in the fall.

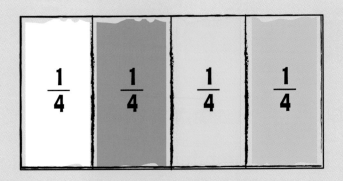

$$\frac{1}{4} = \text{one-fourth}$$

Finishing the Mural

I'm so proud of our class mural. We worked very hard to plan it and paint it. There's something on the mural to represent each of us, and that makes it even more special.

Working on our class mural taught me about teamwork and **cooperation**. It also taught me that math can be used to help people create beautiful works of art.

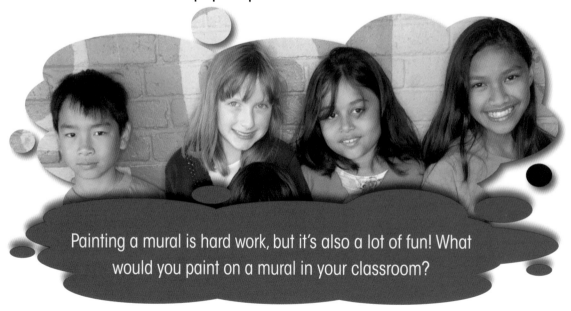

Painting a mural is hard work, but it's also a lot of fun! What would you paint on a mural in your classroom?

Glossary

cooperation (koh-ah-puh-RAY-shun) The act of working together.

creative (kree-AY-tihv) Showing imagination.

divide (duh-VYD) To break into parts or shares.

favorite (FAY-vuh-ruht) Liked best.

project (PRAH-jehkt) A task.

represent (reh-prih-ZEHNT) To stand for something else.

straight (STRAYT) Not bending or curving, always moving in the same direction.

Index

art, 4, 22

circles, 6, 8, 10, 12, 14

corners, 14

equal parts, 8, 10, 12, 18, 20

equal shares, 6, 20

fourths, 12, 20

halves, 8, 10, 12, 16, 20

lines, 6, 8, 14, 16, 18

rectangles, 14, 16, 18, 20

round, 6

sides, 8, 14, 16, 18

thirds, 10, 18

wall, 4, 6

whole, 8, 10, 12, 16

Due to the changing nature of Internet links, The Rosen Publishing Group, Inc., has developed an online list of websites related to the subject of this book. This site is updated regularly. Please use this link to access the list: www.powerkidslinks.com/mm/geo/cmur